A Christmas Carol

by Charles Dickens

CEFR level B1

**Adapted by Karen Kovacs
for
Read Stories – Learn English**

Read Stories – Learn English

A Christmas Carol: CEFR level B1 (ELT Graded Reader)
Original text by Charles Dickens
Illustrations by John Leech
Adapted text © Karen Kovacs, 2024
Logo © Karen Kovacs, 2024

No part of this book may be reproduced, scanned or distributed in any printed or electronic form without permission. Please do not participate in or encourage piracy of copyrighted materials in violation of the author's rights. Thank you for respecting the hard work of the author.

CONTENTS

What are graded readers?   Page 4

Meet the author   Page 5

People in the story   Page 7

The story   Page 9

Exercises   Page 91

More stories   Page 92

Words from the story   Page 94

WHAT ARE GRADED READERS?

Graded readers are books in easy English. They are written for learners of English and use **vocabulary and grammar at your level**.

Each book also includes some new, more difficult words. There are **definitions** for these words at the back of the book.

WHY READ GRADED READERS?

- Studies show that learners who read in English **improve in all areas much faster** than learners who don't read.

- You **don't need a dictionary** so reading is **relaxing**.

- The stories are all in **modern English**.

- You learn vocabulary and grammar **in context** (this is the best way, according to teachers).

- Reading a book in English improves your **comprehension**, **fluency** and **confidence**.

- Graded readers are not exercises. They are **real stories** you can enjoy, helping you **learn English naturally**.

Meet
the author

I'm Karen, a writer from England.

I have a Degree in English Literature and a Master's in Linguistics. I've taught English in the UK and abroad.

I speak Hungarian, French and Spanish, so I understand how it feels to learn a new language.

I hope you enjoy this book.

Karen Kovacs

ReadStories-LearnEnglish.com

Other stories at the same level

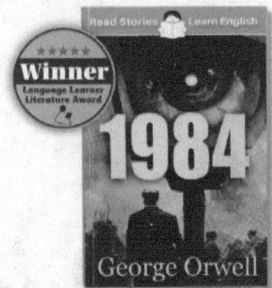
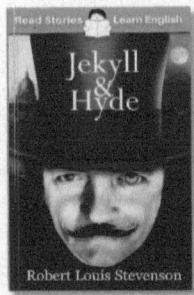

New words

When you see a word in **bold**, go to the back of the book. There you will find a definition of the word.

People in the story

Ebenezer Scrooge

Jacob Marley, Scrooge's former business **partner**

Bob Cratchit, Scrooge's **clerk**

Tiny Tim, Bob's son

Fred, Scrooge's nephew

The Ghost of Christmas Past

The Ghost of Christmas Present

The Ghost of Christmas Future

Chapter 1
Ebenezer Scrooge

Marley was dead. There is no doubt about that. Scrooge had gone to his **funeral**. The priest had added his name to the death register. His body was buried in the churchyard. Yes, Marley was definitely dead.

Did Scrooge know that he was dead? Of course he did. Scrooge and he were **partners** for many years and Scrooge was his only friend.

There is no doubt that Marley was dead. This must be perfectly understood from the beginning or nothing wonderful can come of the story I am going to tell you. If we were not completely sure that Hamlet's father died before the play started, it would not seem amazing that he went for a walk at night, on the walls around his own castle.

Scrooge never removed old Marley's name. It was still there, years afterwards, above the office door: Scrooge and Marley. The firm was known as Scrooge and Marley. Sometimes new customers called Scrooge 'Scrooge' and sometimes 'Marley'. But he didn't care.

Oh! But he was **stingy**, Scrooge! He was really stingy

and as hard as a stone! His heart was so cold that it froze his face and his body. It made his eyes red and his thin lips blue. When he came into a room, it felt immediately colder.

It didn't matter whether it was hot or cold because the weather had no effect on Scrooge. Warm weather couldn't make him warmer; cold weather couldn't make him colder. No wind that blew was colder than him. And no freezing snow or heavy rain was more unpleasant than he was.

Nobody ever stopped him in the street to say, with a smile, "My **dear** Scrooge, how are you? When will you come to see me?" No children asked him for the time, no man or woman ever once in his life asked him for directions to anywhere. Even blind men's dogs appeared to know him and, when they saw him coming, they pulled their owners away from him.

But Scrooge didn't care! In fact, he liked it! He didn't want people to walk up to him and try to talk to him. Not at all!

Once upon a time, on the 24th of December, Christmas Eve, old Scrooge sat busy in his office. It was terribly cold and it was foggy. He could hear the people outside coughing and **rubbing** their hands together to stay warm. The city clocks had only just **struck** three but it was dark already – it hadn't been light all day. Candles were burning in the windows of the other offices in the street, although you could hardly see them in the brown air.

The fog came through every gap and keyhole, and it was so thick that, although the street wasn't very wide, the offices opposite looked like ghosts. The fog hid everything.

The door of the main office, Scrooge's office, was open so that he could watch his **clerk**, who was copying letters in a tiny room. Scrooge had a very small fire, but the clerk's fire was even smaller. For that reason, the clerk was wearing his scarf and was trying to get warm at the candle. But of course that didn't work.

"**Merry** Christmas, Uncle!" cried a cheerful voice. It was the voice of Scrooge's nephew, Fred, who had come into the office without any warning.

"**Bah humbug**!" said Scrooge.

This nephew was so warm from walking quickly in the fog that he was **glowing**. His face was red and handsome, and his eyes shone.

"You think Christmas is a humbug, Uncle?" said Scrooge's nephew. "You don't mean that, I'm sure."

"I do," said Scrooge. "Merry Christmas? Why are you merry? You're poor."

"Well," answered the nephew happily, "why are you miserable? You're rich."

Scrooge didn't have a good answer to that, so he just said "Bah humbug" again.

"Don't be angry, Uncle," said the nephew.

"What else can I be," replied the uncle, "when I live in a world of fools? Merry Christmas? Stop saying merry Christmas! Christmas for you is just a time for paying bills without money; a time for getting a year older, but not getting any richer. Christmas is a waste of time!"

"Don't say that," the nephew said.

"Listen," the uncle replied seriously, "you celebrate Christmas in your own way, and let me celebrate it in mine."

"Celebrate it?" repeated Scrooge's nephew. "But you don't celebrate it!"

"Let me *not* celebrate it then," said Scrooge. "I don't know why anyone does. Christmas has never **done you any good**!"

"I have never made any money from it, that's true," replied the nephew, "but it *has* done me good. I have always thought that Christmas was a good time, a kind, forgiving, pleasant time, a time for **charity**. It's the only time of the year when men and women open their hearts and think of people less lucky than them. And therefore, Uncle, although Christmas has never made me richer, I believe that it *has* done me good and *will* do me good. And I am grateful for it!"

The clerk in the little room clapped. But he realised straight away that his boss would be annoyed with him so he stopped suddenly.

"If you make another sound," said Scrooge, "you'll 'celebrate' Christmas by losing your job! You're a good speaker," he added, turning to his nephew. "You should be a politician."

"Don't be annoyed, Uncle. Come and have dinner with us tomorrow."

"No," answered Scrooge.

"But why?" cried his nephew. "Why?"

"Why did you get married?" said Scrooge.

"Because I fell in love."

"Because you fell in love!" said Scrooge. "That's the only thing in the world more silly than a merry Christmas. Goodbye!"

"I want nothing from you. Why can't we get on?"

"Goodbye," said Scrooge.

"I'm sorry with all my heart that you won't come to us for Christmas, although we've never argued. But I wanted to try and convince you because it's Christmas, and I'll keep celebrating it whatever happens. So merry Christmas, Uncle!"

"Goodbye!" said Scrooge.

His nephew left the room without an angry word. He stopped at the door to wish the clerk a merry Christmas. Although poor Bob Cratchit was cold, his heart was warmer than Scrooge's.

"He's another crazy one," **muttered** Scrooge. "My clerk, with his tiny salary, and a wife and family, talks about a merry Christmas."

As soon as Fred left and the door closed, it opened again, and two men with friendly faces came in. They were pleasant to look at. They took off their hats and stood in front of Scrooge, with books and papers in their hands.

"Good afternoon. This business is Scrooge and Marley's, is that right?" said one of the men, glancing at his list. "Do I have the pleasure of speaking to Mr Scrooge or Mr Marley?"

"Mr Marley has been dead for seven years," Scrooge replied. "He died exactly seven years ago tonight."

"During the **festive** season, Mr Scrooge," said the man, taking out a pen, "it is even more important to give money to charity. It's a difficult time of year for poor people. Many thousands don't have enough money or food, or a home."

"Aren't there any prisons?" asked Scrooge.

"There are plenty of prisons," said the man, putting his

pen down.

"And the **workhouses**?" asked Scrooge. "Are they still open?"

"Yes, they're still open," replied the man. "I wish they weren't."

"Oh! I was worried, from what you said, that they were all closed," said Scrooge. "I'm very glad to hear it."

"A few of us are asking people for money, which we will use to provide poor people with firewood, meat and drink. How much would you like to give?"

"Nothing!" Scrooge replied. "I don't make myself merry at Christmas and I can't afford to make lazy people merry."

"But many will die if we don't help them."

"It's not a bad thing if they die," said Scrooge. "It will reduce the population."

Seeing that it would be useless to try and convince this man, the two charity men left. Scrooge started working again, feeling very satisfied with himself.

Meanwhile, the fog became thicker and the air became darker. The ancient church tower, whose old **bell** was always looking down at Scrooge through a window, struck the hours in the clouds. The cold became more **biting** but people did their best to stay merry. The shop windows looked cheerful with their beautiful festive decorations.

Holly branches could be seen glowing in the heat of the lamps. Even the street cleaner bought some delicious beef to take home to his thin, hungry wife and baby.

It got foggier and colder. A young boy put his face, blue from the cold, to Scrooge's keyhole and started to sing a Christmas **carol**. He was hoping the old man would give him some money, but at the first sound of:

"We wish you a merry Christmas,

We wish you a …"

Scrooge ran to the door and shouted, "Go away!" to the boy. He ran away in **terror**.

At last, it was time to close the office. Scrooge got up from his chair and told his clerk, who immediately put out his candle and put on his hat.

"You'll want the **day off** tomorrow, I suppose?" said Scrooge.

"If it's convenient, sir."

"It's not convenient," said Scrooge, "and it's not fair. I have to pay you but you won't come to work."

The clerk said that it was only once a year.

"That's not a good excuse for stealing from me every 25th of December!" said his boss, putting on his coat. "But I suppose you must have the whole day off. Be here early the next morning."

The clerk promised that he would and Scrooge walked out, muttering. The office was closed in a few seconds, and the clerk, with only his scarf because he couldn't afford a coat, hurried home. When he arrived, he played **blind man's buff** with his family.

Chapter 2
Marley's ghost

Scrooge started walking home. He lived in a flat that had once belonged to his dead partner. Nobody lived in the building except Scrooge because the other rooms were rented out as offices. The yard at the front of the building was so dark and full of fog that Scrooge had to use his hands to find the entrance.

There was nothing unusual about the **knocker** on the door, except that it was very large. And Scrooge had seen this knocker morning and night for several years. He also was not a man with a strong imagination. It's worth knowing too that Scrooge hadn't thought about Marley at all since he had last mentioned his dead partner that afternoon.

So how can you explain that Scrooge, when he put his key in the lock, saw, instead of a knocker, Marley's face?

Marley's face. It wasn't dark like everything else in the yard. No, it was **lit up** somehow. Its hair moved mysteriously although it was not windy. It **stared** at Scrooge with big eyes and this made it very scary.

As Scrooge looked at it, it was a knocker again.

It would be a lie to say that he was not shocked. But he turned the key in the lock and opened the door. He walked into the hall and lit a candle.

He *did* pause before he shut the door, and he *did* look behind it first, to check that he couldn't see the back of Marley's head. But there was nothing there so he said "Bah humbug!" and closed it loudly.

The noise of the door closing sounded like thunder in the empty building. But Scrooge was not scared by that. He walked up the dark stairs with the candle in his hand.

It was even darker in Scrooge's flat. Before he shut his heavy door, he walked through all the rooms to check that everything was alright. He did that because the thought of the face was still at the back of his mind. There was nobody under the table and nobody in the wardrobe so he closed the door and locked it.

He changed into his **pyjamas** and **slippers**, and sat in front of the fire to eat his simple dinner.

It was a small fire on such a cold night. Scrooge had to sit very close to it to feel even a small amount of heat from it. But he didn't mind that. Small fires were cheap.

Scrooge's mind kept returning to the face of his old partner, Jacob Marley. He saw it in the fire in front of him.

"Humbug!" said Scrooge, annoyed with himself. He got up and walked across the room.

After walking around for a minute or two, he sat down again. As he put his head back, he glanced at a small bell that hung in the room. In the past, it had been used to communicate with the **servants** downstairs. But it wasn't used anymore.

Scrooge was very surprised and also terrified when this bell started to move. It moved slowly at first, so slowly that it hardly made a sound. But soon it rang loudly, and so did every other bell in the house. Ding, dong! Ding, dong!

This probably lasted half a minute or a minute, but it seemed like an hour. The bells stopped as they had started – together.

A few seconds later, Scrooge heard another strange noise. What was it? It was coming from deep, deep inside the building. It was coming from the **cellar**. Was it the sound of someone **dragging** a heavy chain across the floor? Scrooge remembered that ghosts in old houses were sometimes described as dragging chains.

The cellar door opened loudly, and the noise started coming up the stairs and straight towards the door to Scrooge's flat.

"Humbug!" said Scrooge. "I won't believe it."

However, his face went white when it came through the heavy door and into the room before his eyes. As it came in, the fire jumped up. It looked like the fire was saying, "I know him. It's Marley's ghost!"

It was the same face, the same clothes and the same boots. But now Marley had a chain around the middle of his body.

Though Scrooge saw the ghost standing before him, though he felt his blood go cold when the ghost looked at him with its cold eyes, he still didn't want to believe that it was real.

"What do you want with me?" said Scrooge, his voice annoyed.

"A lot." It was Marley's voice, no doubt.

"Who are you?"

"Ask me who I *was*."

"Who *were* you?" said Scrooge.

"In life, I was your partner, Jacob Marley," said the ghost.

"Can you, erm … can you sit down?" asked Scrooge. He wasn't sure whether ghosts could sit in chairs.

"I can."

"Do it, then."

The ghost sat down on the opposite side of the fire, like it was a completely normal thing for a ghost to do.

"You don't believe in me, do you?" noticed the ghost.

"No, I don't," said Scrooge.

"You can see me so how is it possible that you don't believe in me?"

"People see things that aren't really there sometimes," said Scrooge. "Your imagination can play tricks on you."

While they were talking, the ghost's hair and clothes were moving a little. It looked like a wind was moving them but there was no wind.

Scrooge looked at the ghost again. "I don't believe it!" cried Scrooge. "Humbug!"

When it heard this, the ghost made a terrible cry and shook its chain.

Scrooge fell to his knees and held his hands before his face.

"I'm sorry," he said. "I *do* believe in you. I do! But tell me – why do you have that chain?"

"I made it during my life," the ghost said. "I made every metre of it. Does it look familiar to you?"

Scrooge **trembled**.

"You have a chain too, although it's **invisible** to you," continued Marley's ghost. "Do you know how long it is? It was as long and as heavy as mine seven years ago. And now it's even longer."

Scrooge glanced down at his body, looking for the chain, but he could see nothing.

"People who weren't good to others in life," said the ghost, "are punished after death. They have a huge chain and they have to travel without rest, dragging it around."

"You've been dead for seven years," said Scrooge gently,

"and you've been travelling all that time?"

"Yes," replied his old partner. "And I regret very much that I wasn't a good person."

"You were a good businessman, Jacob," said Scrooge quietly. He was thinking of himself too when he said this.

"A good businessman!" cried the ghost. "Ha! But I didn't care about other people or try to help them."

Scrooge trembled more and more.

"Listen!" shouted the ghost. "My time is nearly over."

"I'm listening," said Scrooge.

"I don't know why you can see me tonight," said Marley's ghost. "I have sat beside you many nights but you didn't see me."

That was not a pleasant thought.

"I'm here tonight to warn you," continued the ghost. "You still have a chance to change, Ebenezer."

"Thank you, Marley," said Scrooge.

"You will be visited by three ghosts," his old partner told him.

Scrooge looked disappointed when he heard this. "I'd rather not."

"Without their visits," said the ghost, "you will be miserable like me after death. Expect the first ghost tomorrow, when the clocks strike one."

"Can't I see them all together, at the same time?" asked Scrooge.

But the ghost didn't answer him.

"Expect the second on the next night, at the same time. The third will come when the clocks strike midnight. You won't see me again, but remember what I've said."

When it had said these words, the ghost walked backwards. With every step, the window behind him raised a little more. When the ghost reached it, it was completely open.

It showed with its hand that it wanted Scrooge to approach, so Scrooge did.

Suddenly, Scrooge heard noises in the air, sad cries of pain and regret. The ghost, after listening for a moment, started making the same strange sound. Then it floated out into the dark night.

Scrooge went to the window and looked out.

The air was full of ghosts, moving here and there, crying strangely. They all had chains like Marley's ghost and Scrooge recognised some of them. He had known them when they were alive.

These creatures slowly disappeared and the night sky was empty again.

Scrooge closed the window and walked to the main door

of his flat. He looked carefully at it. It was still locked. He started to say "Humbug!" but stopped.

He felt very tired from the conversation with the ghost and because it was so late. He needed to rest so he went straight to bed and fell asleep immediately.

Chapter 3
The first of the three ghosts

When Scrooge woke up, it was really dark. Was it night or day? He looked around but he wasn't sure. He was trying to see into the **darkness**, when he heard the nearby church bell strike six.

Now at least he knew the time. But the clock didn't stop. After striking six o'clock, it struck seven, then eight, and continued until twelve. Twelve! The clock was wrong.

Scrooge took out his pocket watch to check the time. That also showed twelve o'clock.

"That's not possible," said Scrooge. "Have I slept through a whole day and into another night? It can't be twelve noon because there's no sunlight."

The idea was a shocking one. Scrooge got quickly out of bed and went to the window. There was some **frost** on it so he rubbed that off. He looked out but it was still very foggy. He couldn't see anything and there was no noise of people hurrying through the streets. During the day, he could always hear people below.

Scrooge went back to bed, and thought and thought and

thought. He didn't understand what was happening. The more he thought, the more confused he was.

His mind kept going back to Marley's ghost. Every time he decided that it had all been a dream, his mind returned to the question: was it a dream or not?

Scrooge lay in bed thinking until a quarter to one, when he suddenly remembered that the ghost had warned him of a visit when the clock struck one.

He waited but those fifteen minutes seemed long and he fell asleep again.

At last, he heard the clock. The sound was slow and sad. "Ding, dong."

Immediately afterwards, a strong light lit up the room. Scrooge had curtains around his bed to keep the heat in. He now saw that a hand was pulling apart these curtains – not the curtains at his feet but the ones by his face. As Scrooge looked in terror, he saw a face close to his, a ghost's face.

It was a strange creature. It was like a child because it was the size of a child. But it was also like an old man because its long hair was white. Its arms were thin but strong, and it wore a white **robe**. It held a branch of holly leaves in its hand, but at the same time, its robe was decorated with summer flowers.

The strangest thing was the **crown** on its head. From this crown shone a bright light, which lit up the whole room. No doubt this was why it held under its other arm a large candle **snuffer**, which looked a bit like a hat.

Actually, even this was not the strangest thing about the ghost. Its robe shone in one part and then in another. One bit of its body was light one moment and at another time it was dark. Its appearance kept changing before Scrooge's eyes. One second, it had one leg; the next second, it had twenty. It had a pair of legs without a head, then it had a head without a body.

Scrooge could not get a clear idea of what the ghost looked like in the **gloom**.

"Are you the ghost whose visit I was told about?" asked Scrooge.

"I am."

The voice was soft and gentle.

"Who or what are you?" Scrooge asked.

"I am the Ghost of Christmas Past."

"The past long ago?" said Scrooge.

"No. Your past."

Scrooge asked why the ghost had come.

"I came to help you!" said the ghost.

Scrooge thanked the creature but couldn't help thinking that a good night's sleep would do him more good than this visit.

The ghost seemed to hear Scrooge's thoughts because it said immediately, "Get up and walk with me!"

Scrooge didn't want to go. It was freezing, it was late, his bed was warm, and he was wearing only his pyjamas and slippers. But the ghost took his hand and guided Scrooge to the window.

"I'm a human," Scrooge said, worried. "I'll fall."

"Touch my hand," said the ghost, "and you will be lifted into the air."

As the words were spoken, they passed through the wall and stood on an open country road, with fields on both sides. London had completely **vanished**. The darkness and the fog had vanished with it. It was a clear, frosty winter day, with snow on the ground.

"Oh!" said Scrooge, suddenly delighted as he looked around. "I grew up in this place. I was a boy here!"

The ghost **gazed at** him kindly.

Scrooge could smell a thousand smells floating in the air, each one reminding him of a thousand thoughts, hopes and worries that he had forgotten a long, long time ago!

"Your lip is trembling!" said the ghost. "And is that a tear on your cheek?"

Scrooge muttered that it was nothing. Then he said,

"Where will you lead me?"

"Do you know the way?" asked the ghost.

"Of course!" cried Scrooge, **enthusiastically**. "I could walk it with a **blindfold** on."

They walked along the road, Scrooge recognising every gate and tree, until a little town appeared before them, with its bridge, its church and its river.

Next, they saw some small horses coming towards them with boys on their backs. All these boys were in a great mood and shouted to each other cheerfully, until the wide fields were full of merry music!

"These are only shadows of the things that existed," said the Ghost. "They don't know we're here. We're invisible to them."

The happy travellers came past Scrooge, and he recognised and named every one. Why was he so delighted to see them? Why did his heart beat happily when they called "Merry Christmas!" to each other as they rode back to their homes? Scrooge hated Christmas. It had never done him any good!

They left the road and went inside a school. The classroom was long, gloomy and cold, with hardly any furniture. There were lots of desks but that was all.

The classroom was empty except for one boy, who sat at

a desk reading, completely alone. He was sat close to a fire, but it was too small to make the boy feel warmer. He looked miserable and hungry.

Scrooge sat down at a desk and cried. He cried to see his younger **self**, as he used to be.

"That's you," said the ghost gently. "All your friends have left you and you are alone."

"Yes," answered Scrooge, sadly.

There were mice in the walls and Scrooge heard them moving. There were trees outside, blowing in the wind, and Scrooge heard them although the branches were without leaves. Scrooge heard all these soft sounds and they touched his heart and made him cry even more.

The ghost touched his arm and pointed to his younger self, who was still reading. Suddenly, the older Scrooge saw a man outside the window.

"It's Robinson Crusoe!" shouted Scrooge. "And there's Robinson Crusoe's parrot, with his bright green and yellow body."

The character and the bird from young Scrooge's book were alive in his imagination, so they had become real. Old Scrooge was so excited to see them that he laughed and jumped up and down. The other businessmen in the city would be very surprised to see him like that.

But his mood quickly changed again. Scrooge looked at his former self, said, "Poor boy!" and started crying once more.

A minute later, Scrooge dried his eyes and muttered, "I wish …" He didn't finish his sentence. "But it's too late now."

"Too late for what?" asked the ghost.

"There was a boy singing a Christmas carol at my door yesterday evening. I wish I had given him some money, that's all."

The ghost smiled kindly and then waved its hand. "Let's see another Christmas!"

The young Scrooge became bigger and the room a little darker and dirtier. Some of the windows were broken now. All the other boys had gone home for the festive season but young Scrooge was alone again.

He wasn't reading this time – he was walking up and down the room.

Suddenly the door opened and a little girl, much younger than the boy, ran in. She put her arms around his neck and kissed him many times. She called him her "dear, dear brother".

"I've come to bring you home, dear brother!" said the child, clapping her tiny hands and laughing.

"Home?" answered the boy.

"Yes!" said the child, full of happiness. "Home forever! Father is much kinder than he used to be so home is a happier place now. I'm not scared of him anymore so I asked him if you could come home. And he said yes and told me to come and get you. You'll never come back here." She hugged her brother again. "Oh, Ebenezer, we're going to have a fantastic Christmas together!"

She started to drag him towards the door and he was very willing to accompany her.

They heard a terrible voice in the hall and it filled them with terror. The voice was saying to a servant, "Bring down Ebenezer Scrooge's suitcase from his bedroom!" The next moment, the headteacher appeared. He stared at Scrooge angrily, although he was angry for no reason. Scrooge and his sister looked up at him, afraid.

The headteacher invited the children into his private sitting room. It was extremely cold and there was frost on the insides of the windows.

The strict, serious headteacher took out some drink and a big cake. He gave some to the children. They felt very nervous but they politely ate and drank what the headteacher offered them, although they were trembling.

They saw from the window that the servant had now

brought down Scrooge's suitcase. They were pleased to have this excuse to leave the headteacher's freezing cold sitting room.

They said goodbye and left the school for the last time, laughing and joking together on the journey home.

"She had such a kind heart," said the ghost.

"Yes, she did," said Scrooge. "You're right."

"She died, didn't she?" said the ghost. "But first she grew up and had a child."

"One child," Scrooged answered.

"Your nephew, Fred!" cried the ghost.

Scrooge felt suddenly **unsettled**. He replied quietly, "Yes."

Chapter 4
Happy memories

Although Scrooge and the ghost had only just left the school, they were now in the busy streets of a city, where the shadows of passengers passed by and they could see the shadows of shops, decorated for Christmas. It was evening and the streets were lit up.

The ghost stopped at a certain office building and asked Scrooge if he recognised it.

"Of course I do!" said Scrooge. "I was an **apprentice** here!"

They went in. When Scrooge saw a middle-aged man sat at a high desk, he cried in great excitement, "That's Fezziwig, my old boss! He's alive again!"

Old Fezziwig put down his pen and looked up at the clock, which showed that it was seven o'clock. He rubbed his hands together merrily and laughed loudly. Then he shouted in a big, friendly, cheerful voice, "Hey, Ebenezer! Richard!"

Scrooge's former self, a young man now, came quickly

into the room, accompanied by another apprentice.

"That's Richard Wilkins!" said Scrooge to the ghost. "Yes, there he is! We were good friends."

"Come here, my boys!" said Fezziwig. "Don't work any more tonight. It's Christmas Eve, Richard. It's Christmas Eve, Ebenezer. Let's make some room." He clapped his hands loudly. "Move the desks to the side of the room."

"Alright!" cried his enthusiastic young apprentices.

You wouldn't believe how quickly the young Scrooge and Richard moved all the furniture. It only took them a few minutes. They were as fast as race-horses.

"Move the chairs too, Ebenezer, Richard," shouted Fezziwig. "We need lots of room!"

There was nothing the young men would not move for old Fezziwig. It was done in a minute. They cleaned the floors as well and lit all the lamps. And they made a big fire. Soon the office was warm, dry and cosy, a lovely place to be on that winter's night.

A musician joined them with a music book and went to the front of the room. Then Mrs Fezziwig came in, a huge smile on her face. Then the three Fezziwig daughters came in, laughing and smiling. Then six young men joined the group – they were in love with the Fezziwig girls. All the employees of the business came in too, as well as the cook and her brother.

Some came in shyly, some confidently, some pushing, some pulling! But they all came in and they were all welcome.

So many people! Then they all started dancing, twenty couples at once. They danced for hours! Some danced wonderfully, and some danced terribly, but it didn't matter.

Old Fezziwig clapped his hands and the dancing stopped. "Well done!" he shouted cheerfully. This gave the musician a break – he needed it because he was exhausted. He started drinking a huge glass of beer but Fezziwig immediately started dancing again. Poor musician! He had to start playing again and didn't get another break after that.

Fezziwig and his wife were brilliant and enthusiastic dancers. Their legs moved so quickly, their guests could hardly see them.

There was more dancing, there was cake, there was roast beef, there were pies and plenty of beer. They played games too, then they ate and drank some more. And then they danced again!

When the clock struck eleven, the party ended. Mr and Mrs Fezziwig stood on either side of the door and shook hands with every person as they went out, wishing them all a merry Christmas. When everyone had left except the two apprentices, the Fezziwigs wished them a merry Christmas too. Then the young men went to their beds, in a room at the back of the office.

During this whole time, Scrooge had behaved like a mad person. His whole heart was in the scene and with his former self. He enjoyed everything, remembered everything and felt so happy and excited!

He only remembered the ghost when the two apprentices left the room. He saw then that the ghost was staring at him. And he noticed that the light from the ghost's head shone very brightly.

"Everyone loves Fezziwig," said the ghost, "but does he deserve it? After all, he didn't do much. He only organised a little party and spent a few pounds." But the ghost smiled as it talked. It was testing its 'pupil'.

Scrooge didn't notice the smile and got annoyed with the ghost. He spoke like his younger self, not his older self. "Maybe it wasn't a huge party, but that's not what matters," he said. "He was a fun, kind man and he made us all happy! He made us so happy!"

The ghost glanced at him and he stopped talking.

"What's the matter?" asked the ghost.

"Nothing," answered Scrooge.

"Something is wrong. Tell me," the ghost said.

"I would just like to be able to say a word or two to my clerk right now. That's all," said Scrooge.

The next moment, Scrooge and the ghost were standing next to each other in the street.

"My time is nearly over," said the ghost. "We must hurry!"

The scene changed again. Now, Scrooge saw himself a

few years older. His face didn't look as **carefree** anymore. He seemed unsettled and also less kind than before.

He was not alone. He sat next to a young woman, who had tears in her eyes. They glowed in the light that shone from the crown of the Ghost of Christmas Past.

"You've changed," said the woman gently. "You prefer something else to me now."

"Something else?" asked the young Scrooge, confused.

"Money!" said the woman. "You only care about money. We got engaged when we were younger and poor. We didn't mind being poor and we were happy. But you were a different person then."

"But I still love you, Belle," said the young Scrooge.

"Your heart is becoming colder," she said sadly. "You love me less and less, and you love money more and more. We should split up."

"Why?" he asked, shocked.

"Be honest," she explained. "If you met me now, at this period in your life, would you ask me to marry you?"

She glanced at him and saw the truth in his face. "No," she said, "you wouldn't. I'm poor. You would choose a rich woman now."

She got up and spoke to him one last time. "I hope you are happy with the life you have chosen." And then she left him.

"Don't show me any more!" said Scrooge. "Take me home! Why do you enjoy **torturing** me?"

"I want to show you one more thing," said the ghost.

"No more!" cried Scrooge.

But the ghost didn't listen. There were now in another place. It was a room, not very large, but very cosy. Near the fire, there was a beautiful young girl. She looked so similar to the woman from the last scene that Scrooge thought it was the same person. But then an older woman came into the room and sat opposite her daughter.

The room was noisy because there were more children too but nobody minded. In fact, the mother and daughter laughed and enjoyed it very much.

Suddenly, there was a knock at the front door and everyone hurried to greet the father of the family. His hands were full of Christmas presents. The children hugged him and tried to grab the presents.

An hour later, the younger children went upstairs to bed and the couple were on their own with only the older daughter. This daughter sat down with her father by the fire, her arm around him.

Scrooge watched them and thought sadly, "She would be my daughter but I split up with her mother."

"Belle," said the husband, turning to his wife with a smile, "I saw an old friend of yours this afternoon."

"Who was it?"

"Guess!"

"How can I? I don't know!" She laughed as he laughed. Then she said, "Mr Scrooge."

"Yes, that's right. It was Mr Scrooge. I passed his office window. There was a candle inside so I couldn't help seeing him. People say that his partner, Marley, is dying. And Scrooge sat there alone … alone in the world."

"Ghost!" said Scrooge, trying not to cry. "Take me away from this place."

"I told you these were shadows of the things that were," said the ghost. "If they make you sad, don't blame me!"

He turned to the ghost and saw that it was staring at him. The light from its crown was shining brightly.

"Stop torturing me!" Scrooge shouted. "Take me away! I can't stand it!"

The ghost didn't answer him and Scrooge got angry. He thought that maybe he could put out that light, and then the ghost would go away. So he grabbed the snuffer from the ghost's hand and quickly pushed it down onto its head.

Soon the snuffer covered the ghost's whole body. However, although Scrooge pressed down very hard, he couldn't hide the ghost's light. It still shone on the ground from under the snuffer.

Scrooge was exhausted and felt suddenly very sleepy. He wanted to be back in his own bedroom.

The next moment, he was in his bed and sleeping heavily.

Chapter 5
The second of the three ghosts

When Scrooge woke up, it was nearly one o'clock again. He was ready to meet the second ghost sent by Jacob Marley. But he did not want this ghost to pull apart the bed curtains by his head, like the last ghost did. That was too scary. So Scrooge opened the bed curtains himself and then lay back down.

Scrooge looked around him, waiting for the ghost to appear. After the last time, he was prepared for something strange. A baby or even an elephant would not surprise him!

However, he was not prepared for nothing. That was why, when the bell struck one and no creature appeared, he started trembling. Five minutes, ten minutes, a quarter of an hour passed, but nothing came.

All this time, as he lay on his bed, there was a strong light shining onto it. This light started to shine at exactly one o'clock. Scrooge was more unsettled by this strange light than by a dozen ghosts because he didn't understand what it meant. He wondered whether the light would burn him!

At last, he realised that the ghostly light might be coming from the next room. It seemed to shine from that direction. This idea filled his mind and he got up softly and moved slowly in his slippers to the door.

As soon as Scrooge's hand was on the door, a strange voice called his name and told him to enter. He did what the voice told him.

It was his own room. There was no doubt about that. But it was completely **altered**. The walls and ceiling were decorated with holly branches so that the room looked like a wood! The leaves were like little mirrors – the light shone on the leaves and then shone back into the room. And there was a huge fire! There had never been a fire as big as that in Scrooge's time, or Marley's.

On the floor, there were piles of turkeys, **geese**, chickens, pigs, sausages, **puddings**, pies, red apples, juicy oranges and pears, large cakes, and bowls of hot **mulled wine**.

All this made a sort of huge seat, and on this seat there was a cheerful **giant**. It was wonderful to see. It was holding a glowing **torch**, high above its head. The light from this torch shone on Scrooge as he glanced around the door.

"Come in!" cried the giant ghost enthusiastically. "Come in and let's get to know each other!"

Scrooge entered, feeling very shy and looking down at

the ground. Scrooge was not the confident man he used to be and, although the ghost's eyes were clear and kind, he didn't want to look into them.

"I am the Ghost of Christmas Present," said the ghost. "Look at me!"

To show his respect to this giant, Scrooge looked up at it. It was wearing a simple green robe, bordered with white fur. The robe was so loose that it hung open and Scrooge could see the whole of the top part of the giant's body.

Under the folds of the robe, Scrooge could see its feet. It wasn't wearing any shoes. The only thing on its head were branches of Christmas holly. Its dark brown, curly hair was long and free. Its face was friendly and its eyes shone happily.

"You've never seen anything like me before!" cried the ghost.

"Never," Scrooge answered.

The Ghost of Christmas Present got up.

"Ghost," said Scrooge quietly because he was still feeling shy, "take me wherever you like. I went out last night without wanting to and I learnt an important lesson. Tonight, if you have anything to teach me, I am ready to learn."

"Touch my robe!"

Scrooge did as he was told and held it in his hand.

Holly, turkeys, geese, chickens, pigs, sausages, puddings,

pies, fruit, cakes and mulled wine all vanished. So did the room, the fire, the glow, the hour of night.

They now stood in the city streets on Christmas morning. It was frosty and the cold was biting. The people made a rough but pleasant sort of music, by removing the snow from the pavement in front of their houses and from the tops of their roofs. Crowds of little boys watched as they did this. They were delighted when the snow fell down onto the road and made big, soft piles.

The houses looked black and the windows blacker next to the bright white snow on the roofs and on the ground. The sky was gloomy and the smaller streets were full of fog, half frozen. There was nothing very cheerful in the city but there was a cheerful mood in the air. The mood would not be more cheerful even on a warm summer's day.

Why? Because the people who were removing the snow from their homes were happy and smiling. They shouted to each other from the roofs and sometimes threw snowballs at each other. Then they laughed merrily.

The shops were still open and wonderfully decorated. There were huge baskets of food at the doors full of brown onions and shiny apples. There were grapes hung from the ceilings, and piles of oranges and lemons on the floor. Customers bought them and carried them home in paper bags to be eaten after dinner.

Other shops sold tea and coffee, and rare spices. They sold dried fruit in beautifully decorated boxes. Some of the customers were hurrying so much that they left their items in the shop by mistake. They came running back to fetch them, laughing and saying, "Oh, silly me!"

The customers were all cheerful and all keen to get home quickly, so that the Christmas celebrations could begin!

Other people heard the bells and went to their local church in their best clothes and with happy, glowing faces.

At the same time, from many smaller streets, lots and lots of poor people appeared. They were carrying their dinners to bakers' shops. They did this because they were too poor to own their own ovens. They took the food to these shops and the baker baked their meals for them.

The Ghost of Christmas Present seemed especially interested in these people. He stood at the entrance to the bakers' shops and, from his torch, he **sprinkled** water onto their food.

It was a very special torch because, once or twice, when some of these poor people got angry with each other and started to argue, he sprinkled magic water on their dinners and they were immediately in a good mood again! "It's a shame to argue on Christmas Day!" they said

"Is your torch magic?" asked Scrooge.

"Yes, it is," answered the ghost.

"Would you use it on any dinner today?" asked Scrooge.

"Yes, but especially on a poor dinner."

"Why especially on a poor dinner?" asked Scrooge.

"Because it needs it most."

They continued walking, invisible to everyone, as they had been before. They reached a different part of the city and went into various shops and houses. It was amazing to see that, although the giant was huge, he could fit into any room, even if it had a low ceiling.

Before long, the ghost's generous heart and his special love for poor people took him to the home of Scrooge's clerk. Scrooge went with him, holding his robe.

At the entrance, the ghost stopped and sprinkled water from his torch. He was **blessing** it. The ghost was blessing Bob Cratchit's tiny house!

They went inside and saw Mrs Cratchit, Bob Cratchit's wife. She was wearing a **shabby** dress because the family never had enough money. But the house was clean and Mrs Cratchit tried to make everything look pretty.

Her second daughter, Belinda Cratchit, was helping her. Peter Cratchit, her oldest, stood over a saucepan of potatoes with a fork in his hand and stole a potato when no one was looking.

And now two smaller Cratchits, a boy and a girl, hurried in, screaming that outside the baker's they had smelt the goose … *their* goose for *their* Christmas meal! The baker was cooking it for them because the family didn't have an oven. They danced around the table happily.

"Where is your dad, I wonder?" said Mrs Cratchit. "And your brother, Tiny Tim? And Martha is late again, like last Christmas Day!"

"I'm here, Mum!" said a girl, appearing as she spoke.

"Martha's here, Martha's here!" cried the two young Cratchits. "Martha, the goose smells amazing!"

"My dear girl, you are so late!" said Mrs Cratchit, kissing her a dozen times.

"We had a load of work to finish this morning," replied the oldest daughter.

"Well, never mind. You're here now," said Mrs Cratchit. "Sit by the fire and get warm!"

"No, no! Dad's coming!" cried the two young Cratchits. "Hide, Martha, hide!"

So Martha hid herself and Bob, the father, came in with over a metre of scarf hanging round his neck and over his shabby clothes. And Tiny Tim was on his shoulder. Sadly for Tiny Tim, he was carrying a little **crutch** because his legs were weak.

"Where's Martha?" cried Bob Cratchit, looking round.

"She's not coming," said Mrs Cratchit.

"Not coming!" said Bob, and he suddenly became sad. "She's not coming on Christmas Day?"

Martha didn't like to see him disappointed, although it was only a joke, so she came out from behind the cupboard door. She ran into his arms and they both laughed. Meanwhile, the two young Cratchits showed Tiny Tim the Christmas pudding, which was boiling in a saucepan. They all listened as it made a singing sound.

"Did Tiny Tim behave well in church?" Mrs Cratchit asked her husband, who stopped hugging his daughter to answer.

"Oh, yes. He behaved brilliantly." Bob's voice trembled as he added, "He's growing stronger and more healthy."

The parents heard the little crutch on the floor and Tiny Tim came back before another word was spoken. His brother and sister took the boy to his little seat by the fire while Bob stirred the mulled wine.

Peter Cratchit and the two young Cratchits went to fetch the goose from the baker's shop and came back with it.

Everyone was so happy to see it! It was nothing special – it was only an ordinary goose. But to them, it was everything.

Belinda had made an apple sauce for it and she took it to the table. Bob took Tiny Tim to a tiny corner of the table, beside him. Mrs Cratchit took a huge knife and cut up the bird. All the children hit the backs of their knives on the table enthusiastically and cried, "Yay! Yay!"

It was the best goose in the world, or at least that's what the Cratchit family believed. It was the tastiest, biggest bird ever! It's true that it was quite big. Everyone had enough to eat.

When they had finished eating, Mrs Cratchit got up to fetch the Christmas pudding. The family were worried. What if it wasn't big enough? What if it broke when their mother took it out of the dish? What if it was hard?

Mrs Cratchit returned to the table with the pudding, smiling proudly. She had decorated it with holly and poured alcohol over it. She had lit the alcohol and now it was burning brightly.

It was a wonderful pudding! Bob Cratchit said it was Mrs Cratchit's biggest success since their marriage. Everybody said it was amazing but nobody said that is was a small pudding for such a large family. They didn't even think it. They would never admit that.

Chapter 6
God bless us, every one!

At last, dinner was over. They cleared the table and went to sit together around the fire. Bob stirred the mulled wine one more time and Mrs Cratchit gave him three cups, one of them broken. That was all they had so they had to share. Bob poured some of the hot drink into each cup and they had a **toast**.

"Merry Christmas to us all, my dears," Bob cried happily. "God bless us!"

The family all repeated his toast.

"God bless us, every one!" said Tiny Tim, the last of all.

He sat very close to his father. Bob held Tony Tim's thin little hand in his. Bob wished to keep his son close always. He was afraid to lose him.

"Ghost," said Scrooge, with an interest he had never felt before, "tell me if Tiny Tim will live."

"I see an empty seat," replied the ghost, "in the corner, and a crutch without an owner. If these shadows are not altered, the child will die."

"No, no," said Scrooge. "Oh, no, kind ghost! Say he'll live."

"Why are you so worried?" replied the ghost. "It's not a bad thing if he dies. It will reduce the population."

Scrooge looked down at the floor, ashamed to hear his own words spoken by the ghost. He regretted now what he had said.

"Listen," said the ghost, "if you have a heart, don't talk like that again. Will you decide who can live and who can die? Maybe you are worth much less than this poor man's child!"

Scrooge's head was still down, and he was trembling. But he raised it when he heard his own name.

"I'd like to toast Mr Scrooge!" said Bob. "Without him, there would be no Christmas meal!"

Mrs Cratchit was annoyed by this. "Why do we have to toast such a rude, nasty, stingy, cold-hearted man? You know he is, Bob! Nobody knows it better than you!"

"My dear," was Bob's gentle answer. "It's Christmas Day. Let's not speak badly of him."

"I'll toast him because you're asking me to and because it's Christmas Day," said Mrs Cratchit. "Merry Christmas and a Happy New Year to Mr Scrooge. He'll be extremely merry and extremely happy, I'm sure!"

The children drank the toast after her. It was the first event that evening that nobody felt enthusiastic about. Nobody in the family liked Scrooge. When his name was mentioned, every Cratchit became miserable. The mood in the room didn't improve for five minutes.

However, when it did improve, it was ten times merrier than before. Bob told them he had found a possible job for Peter and they were all delighted to hear it. Martha told them about her difficult work at the hat shop. She couldn't wait to have a **lie in** the next morning – the next day was a day off for her and she would spend it at home.

Tiny Tim sang a sad little song about a lost child travelling in the snow but he sang it very well.

There was nothing special about the Cratchits. They were not a good-looking family and they were shabby. But they were happy and grateful, and they loved each other.

Just before they left, the giant sprinkled blessings from his torch on the family, while Scrooge watched them all, especially Tiny Tim.

It was getting dark and it was snowing heavily. As Scrooge and the ghost went along the streets, it was wonderful to see the bright fires in the kitchens and the other rooms. Children ran out into the streets to greet their older brothers and sisters. Groups of pretty young women stood together chatting and laughing.

The giant poured his blessings on all of them with a generous hand.

And now, without any warning from the ghost, they stood in a dark, gloomy field. Nothing grew here except rough grass. The sun was going down and it was red like fire. Then it was gone and the sky was black.

"What is this place?" asked Scrooge.

"It's a place where very poor people live," replied the ghost.

A light shone from the window of a hut, and they moved quickly towards it. Passing through the wooden wall, they found a cheerful group sitting around a glowing fire. An old, old man and woman, with their children and their children's children, were all wearing their best clothes. The old man was singing them a Christmas song, in a voice that was rarely louder than the strong, biting wind that blew across the dark, empty field.

It had been a very old song when he was a boy, and sometimes his family all joined in and sang with him.

Scrooge was listening to the singing and to the sad, frightening noise of the wind when, suddenly, he heard a loud laugh. He was surprised by this but he was even more surprised to recognise it as his nephew's laugh. He looked up and saw that he was now in a bright, dry room, with the ghost standing beside him. He was smiling and gazing at Fred.

"Ha, ha!" laughed Scrooge's nephew. "Ha, ha, ha!"

Did you know that you can catch an illness but you can also catch happiness? When Scrooge's nephew laughed in this way, his wife laughed as merrily as him. And all their friends laughed too.

"Ha, ha! Ha, ha, ha, ha!"

"He said that Christmas was a humbug!" cried Scrooge's nephew. "And he believed it!"

"He should be ashamed to talk like that," said the wife, more serious now. She was very pretty and had bright, sunny eyes.

"He's not that nice, that's the truth," said Scrooge's nephew. "But he's my uncle and I won't speak against him."

"He's very rich, isn't he, Fred?" said his wife.

"He is," answered Fred, "but his money does him no good. He doesn't do anything good with it and he doesn't make himself comfortable with it."

"I don't like him," said the wife. Her sisters all agreed with her.

"Oh, I do!" said Scrooge's nephew. "I feel sorry for him.

I couldn't be angry with him if I tried. His bad attitude makes him very miserable. For example, he has decided to dislike us so he won't come and have dinner with us."

They were all sat together around the fire.

Fred continued. "He dislikes us and doesn't visit us so he is missing some really fun moments. I'm sure we could make him happier than his own thoughts! I ask him to join us every year and I will never stop. He can say 'Bah humbug' every Christmas until he dies, but maybe, if I keep going to see him, one day he will feel a little happier."

Soon, they were all laughing again.

They were a musical group and Fred's wife played the piano beautifully. She played and they all sang merrily.

She played a tune that Scrooge knew from his past. His sister used to play it to him. When he heard it, all the things the ghosts had shown him came into his mind, and his heart got softer and softer.

The group didn't spend all evening singing. After a while, they played blind man's buff because it's good to be children sometimes, and never better than at Christmas.

Topper, Fred's friend, had a blindfold on but he was definitely not really 'blind' during the game! He could see a bit although he didn't admit it. He wanted to catch one of the sisters because he was in love with her so he moved around the room following her, the blindfold not completely covering his eyes. Wherever she went, he went too! He didn't catch anybody else! She cried that it wasn't fair and it's true that it wasn't. But everybody just carried on playing.

At the end of the game, Topper and the woman sat in a corner together, smiling and talking quietly. Obviously, she wasn't angry with him at all!

Later, they all played Yes or No. This was a guessing game. Someone thought of something and the others had to guess what it was. The person could only answer yes or no. Fred's wife was really good at this game and Fred was secretly proud of her for it.

All twenty people in the room played, shouting answers, including Scrooge! He forgot that he was invisible and that they couldn't hear him either. His voice made no sound in their ears. It was a shame because he very often guessed correctly. He was a clever man, after all.

The ghost was pleased to see him in this mood. Scrooge **begged** like a boy to stay until the guests left but the ghost said that was not possible.

Soon, Scrooge and the ghost were travelling again. They visited many homes but always with a happy end. The ghost stood beside the beds of people who were ill … and they became cheerful. He went to people who were living abroad … and they felt closer to home. He visited people who were poor … and they felt rich.

He and Scrooge went to hospitals and prisons and, in every place, the giant left his blessing and taught Scrooge his lesson.

It was a long night, but only one night. Actually, Scrooge had his doubts about this. He wasn't sure how could so many things fit into one night.

It was strange too that, although Scrooge's appearance didn't alter, the ghost's did. He became older, clearly older. Scrooge had noticed this change but he never mentioned it until they left a children's Christmas party. Then, looking at the ghost as they stood together in a dark field, he noticed that his hair was grey.

"Is your life that short?" asked Scrooge.

"My life in this world is short," replied the ghost. "It ends tonight."

"Tonight?" cried Scrooge.

"Tonight at midnight," said the ghost. "The time is nearly here."

Scrooge stared at the ghost's robe. After a moment, he said, "What is that under your robe? I think I see something there. Is it the foot of a wild animal?"

"It's a very thin foot, but it doesn't belong to a wild animal," was the ghost's sad reply. "Look."

From the folds in his robe, two children appeared. They looked thin and miserable and frightening. They went down on their knees at the ghost's feet, grabbing his robe with both hands.

"Look," the ghost repeated.

They were a boy and a girl. Their clothes were shabby and they looked unhealthy. They were young, and young children normally have glowing cheeks and happy faces. But these children didn't. They looked older than their age and they looked hungry. In fact, they looked almost like little monsters.

Scrooge moved backwards, shocked. He tried to say they were lovely children but the words stopped in his throat and wouldn't come out. He didn't want to lie.

"Are they yours, ghost?" That was all Scrooge could say.

"They belong to everyone," said the ghost, looking down at them. "They don't want to leave me so they are always with me. They **represent** all the poor people of this city. Their condition represents how difficult life is for poor people. And it shows how rich people don't care about the lives of others, who are not as lucky as them."

"Don't they have anywhere to go?" cried Scrooge, feeling very sorry for them.

"Aren't there any prisons?" said the ghost, using Scrooge's own words from previously. "And the workhouses? Are they still open?"

The bell struck twelve.

Scrooge looked around him for the ghost, but he couldn't see him anymore.

As the bell stopped trembling, he remembered what old Jacob Marley had said. He lifted up his eyes and saw another ghost, dressed in a long robe and wearing a **hood**. It was floating like a **mist** along the ground, towards him.

Chapter 7
The last of the ghosts

The ghost slowly, seriously, silently approached. As it moved towards him, Scrooge went down on his knee because this ghost seemed to bring mystery and gloom with him as he came.

It was dressed in a black robe, which hid its head, its face and its body. Everything was invisible except one hand. This hand was the only thing that made it possible to separate it from the night and from the darkness that surrounded it.

Scrooge noticed that the ghost was tall when it came beside him and that it gave him a feeling of **dread**. He didn't know any more because the ghost didn't speak or move.

"You're the Ghost of Christmas Future, aren't you?" said Scrooge.

The Spirit didn't answer but it pointed forwards with its hand.

"You're about to show me shadows of the things that have not happened but will happen in the future," Scrooge said. "Is that right, ghost?"

The upper part of the robe and hood moved a bit for a moment, as if the ghost had moved its head down and then up again. That was the only answer he received.

Although Scrooge was used to ghosts by this time, this silent shape filled him with terror and made his legs tremble under him. He could hardly stand when he prepared to follow it. The ghost paused a moment because it had noticed Scrooge's difficulty and wanted to give him time to recover.

But this made Scrooge feel even worse. He felt unsettled to know that, behind the dark hood, there were ghost's eyes staring at him while Scrooge, although he tried really hard, could see nothing but a white hand and one great pile of black.

"Ghost of the Future!" he cried. "I'm more scared of you, more than any ghost I've seen. But I know your purpose is to do me good. And I hope to live to be a better man than I was, so I'm prepared to follow you and do it with a grateful heart. Won't you speak to me?"

It gave him no reply. The hand was pointed straight before them.

"Show me the way!" said Scrooge. "The night will soon be over, and every minute matters, I know. Show me the way, ghost!"

The ghost moved away as it had come towards him. Scrooge followed in the shadow of its robe, which seemed to lift him up and carry him along.

They didn't exactly enter the city – instead, the city seemed to appear around them, like magic. They were in the centre of the city, among the businessmen, who hurried left and right, and talked in groups, and looked at their watches, as Scrooge had seen them often.

The ghost stopped beside one little group of businessmen. Seeing that the hand was pointed to them, Scrooge moved towards them and listened to their conversation.

"No," said a great fat man with a huge chin, "I don't know much about it. I only know he's dead."

"When did he die?" asked another.

"Last night, I think."

"What was the matter with him?" asked a third. "I thought he'd never die."

"I have no idea," said the first, looking bored.

"What has he done with his money?" asked a red-faced man with a big nose.

"I haven't heard," said the man with the large chin. "Maybe he's left it to his company. He hasn't left it to me – that's all I know!"

The other men laughed at this joke.

"It's likely to be a very cheap funeral," said the same speaker, "because I don't know anybody who would go to it. Shall we all go?"

"I don't mind going if I'm given a free lunch," said the man with the big nose. "I won't go unless I get lunch."

Everyone laughed again.

"Well, I might go," said the first speaker. "And I have more reason than any of you because we used to stop and speak whenever we met. Bye!"

The speakers and the listeners moved away from each other and mixed with other groups.

Scrooge knew the men and looked towards the ghost for an explanation.

The ghost floated to another street. Its finger pointed to two people. Scrooge listened again, thinking that this conversation might explain things.

He knew these men, too. They were businessmen, very rich and important. He had always wanted them to think well of him – as a businessman only, strictly as a businessman.

"How are you?" said one.

"How are you?" replied the other.

"Well!" said the first. "The old guy has died at last, hey?"

"Yes, I heard," answered the second. Then he started a different topic. "It's cold, isn't it?"

"Yes, but that's normal for Christmas time," said the first man. "Do you enjoy skating?"

"No. No," answered the first man. "I'm too busy for skating. Goodbye!"

They didn't say another word. That was their meeting, their whole conversation.

Scrooge was surprised that the ghost gave so much importance to conversations like that. But he felt sure that there was a hidden meaning. After all, the ghost had made the effort to show him. But why? Scrooge thought hard about it.

The conversations were not about Jacob, his old partner, because that was past and this ghost was showing him the future. And he didn't think they were about anyone else he knew either. Anyway, Scrooge was ready to learn the lesson, when he found out what it was.

He looked carefully for his future self. How would he behave? It would be interesting to see and maybe it would give him the explanation he was looking for.

Scrooge looked for himself but he wasn't there.

Quiet and dark beside him, the ghost pointed again with its hand. It was a little while before Scrooge noticed because he was so busy thinking. But when he did notice, he felt that the ghost's eyes were staring at him. It made him shake with fear and feel very cold.

They left the busy scene and went into a poor part of town, where Scrooge had never been before. The streets were dirty and narrow, and the people were shabby and miserable.

On one of these streets, there was a shop. Here, old clothes, bottles and bones were sold. On the floor, there were piles of old keys, chains and other metal objects. Sitting in the middle of all this, there was a grey-haired man, nearly seventy years old and calmly smoking.

Scrooge and the ghost entered the shop just as a woman with a huge bag went in. A moment later, another woman came as well, with a similar bag.

It was night time and the old man lit a lamp.

The first woman threw her bag on the floor.

"What do you have for me today?" asked the man. "Don't look so afraid. You shouldn't feel bad for taking his things. He won't miss them – he's dead!"

They all laughed.

"You're right," said the woman. "He was lying there alone. He was a stingy, cold-hearted man so nobody was there looking after his body and his stuff."

She opened the bag. "Have a look, Joe, and tell me how much all this is worth."

Joe, the old man, looked at the items. It wasn't much – sheets and towels, some silver teaspoons, a few boots and one piece of jewellery. He added up the total.

Now it was the turn of the other woman. "Look in my bag, Joe."

Joe went down on his knees so that he could open it more easily. He pulled out some dark stuff.

"What's this?" he asked. "Bed curtains?"

"Yes," the woman answered, laughing. "Bed curtains."

"Did you take them down while he was lying there?" said Joe.

"Yes," admitted the woman. "Why not? He wasn't a kind man so why should I feel guilty?"

"You're right," laughed Joe.

"I took his shirt from his body too. Look, there it is," she told him, pointing. "It's a very good-quality shirt and they were going to bury him in it. What a waste!"

Joe gave each woman an amount of money.

The second woman laughed. "Ha! Everyone hated him when he was alive so now we can make money from his stuff after his death. Ha, ha, ha!"

Scrooge listened in shock. This was terrible.

"Ghost!" he said, trembling from head to foot. "I see, I see. If I don't change, the same will happen to me too. Agh, what is this?"

The scene had changed suddenly and now he almost touched a bed, a bed with no curtains. There was something on the bed, under a shabby sheet.

The room was very dark so Scrooge couldn't see anything clearly. But he knew that the thing under the sheet was a body and that nobody was by this man's bed. Nobody was crying for him. He lay in a dark empty house, without family or friends to say that he was kind or that they missed him.

Scrooge glanced towards the ghost. Its hand was pointed to the head. Lifting the sheet would be easy and Scrooge was keen to do it but he was too scared.

"Ghost!" he said. "I understand my lesson. Let's go now!"

But the ghost still pointed to the head.

"I can't!" said Scrooge. "I can't do it."

The ghost seemed to look at him.

"If there is anyone who feels **emotion** about this man's death," said Scrooge, very upset, "show me that person, ghost, please!"

Chapter 8
Feeling grateful

The ghost held its dark robe before them for a moment, like a wing. When it took his robe away, Scrooge saw a room by daylight, where a mother and children were.

She was expecting someone, and she clearly felt worried. She walked up and down the room, jumping at every sound; she looked out of the window; she glanced at the clock; she tried to sew but she couldn't because her mind was too full of thoughts and worries. And she could hardly stand the voices of the children as they played.

At last, the expected knock was heard. She hurried to the door and met her husband. Scrooge could see that he was normally anxious and depressed, although he was young. But his face looked different now. He seemed delighted but, at the same time, he seemed ashamed of feeling delighted and he was trying to hide it.

He sat down to eat the dinner that his wife had prepared for him earlier, and when she asked him for the news (which was not until after a long silence), he appeared embarrassed again and didn't know how to answer.

"Is it good news," she said, "or bad?" She was filled with dread.

"Bad," he answered.

"So we're **bankrupt**?"

"No, we're not bankrupt. There is still hope, Caroline."

"If he changes his mind, there is hope," she said. "But is it possible that he will?"

"He can't change his mind anymore," said her husband. "He's dead."

She was a kind person – you could see it in her face. But she was grateful to hear that he was dead and she said so. The next moment, she hoped that God would forgive her and she was sorry. But the grateful feeling was the first emotion of her heart.

"I tried to see him. I wanted to ask for another week to pay him back the money. His clerk told me that he couldn't see me and I thought it was just an excuse. But in fact it was true. He was not only very ill – he was dying."

"Who will our **debt** be transferred to?" asked his wife. "Who will we owe the money to now?"

"I don't know. But now we have extra time to pay back the debt. And anyway before it's transferred, we will find the money."

"What if we don't?" said his wife, still worried. "I don't want to go to the workhouse!"

"There isn't a man in England with a heart as cold as his was, Caroline," said the husband, "so don't worry. Our debt can't be transferred to a less kind person so we'll be alright, you'll see."

His wife smiled at him.

"We can sleep tonight with light hearts," he told her merrily.

Yes. Although they felt guilty for being happy that someone had died, their hearts *were* lighter. The children's faces, when they came to sit by the fire with their parents, were brighter, although they didn't understand what was going on. It was a happier house because that man had died! The only emotion that the ghost could show Scrooge, involving the event, was pleasure.

"Alright," said Scrooge, his head down. "Nobody feels sad about the death. I understand." He was silent for a moment, then he said, "So instead, please show me someone who feels sad about another person's death."

The ghost led him through several streets that were familiar to him and, as they went along, Scrooge looked here and there to find himself, but he was nowhere.

They entered poor Bob Cratchit's house, the home he had

visited before, and found the mother and the children sat around the fire.

They were all quiet. Very quiet. The noisy little Cratchits were like statues in one corner, not moving, and Peter was reading a book. The mother and her daughters were sewing. Yes, they were all very quiet!

Scrooge thought he saw a tear on Mrs Cratchit's face.

"Dad will be home soon," said Peter, closing his book. "But he walks slower now."

They were quiet again.

Finally, the mother answered. "I saw him walk very quickly with Tiny Tim on his shoulder ... many times."

"Yes, that's true!" cried Peter.

"But he wasn't heavy," she continued, "and your father loved him so much. Oh, there he is at the door!"

She hurried to meet him and Bob came in. He was wearing his long scarf – he needed it, poor man. His dinner was ready for him and they all tried to give it to him. Then the two young Cratchits got up onto their father's knees and they each put a little cheek against his face. They wanted to make him feel better.

Bob tried to be cheerful and spoke pleasantly.

"It's a beautiful place," he told his wife. "The churchyard where they will bury him – it's beautiful and peaceful. I promised him that I would walk there every Sunday. My little, little child!" cried Bob. "My little child!"

He started crying. He couldn't help it.

He left the room and went upstairs into the room above. The room was cheerfully lit and decorated for Christmas. There was a chair beside the child's body and poor Bob sat down on it.

When Bob had thought a little and controlled his emotions, he kissed the little face. He could accept what had happened now and he went downstairs again, feeling quite happy.

The family sat around the fire and talked. The girls and their mother carried on sewing. Bob told them about Scrooge's nephew and how kind he had been that day.

He had only met Fred once or twice before but, when Bob saw him in the street, Fred noticed that Bob looked sad. He asked him what was wrong so Bob told him the sad news. "I'm so sorry, Mr Cratchit," Fred said to him. "And I'm very sorry for your wife. If I can help you in any way, let me know."

"And he gave me his address," Bob told his family. "It seemed that he had known Tiny Tim, although he never met him. He was so kind."

"He's a good person!" said Mrs Cratchit.

Bob spoke again. "One day, you will all leave this house," he said to his children, "but we must all promise one thing. We will never forget Tiny Tim."

"Never, Dad!" they all cried.

"And I'm sure," said Bob, "that we will remember how sweet and gentle he was, although he was only a little, little child, and we won't argue too much. We'll be patient with each other and we'll never forget Tiny Tim."

"Never, Dad!" they all cried again.

Mrs Cratchit kissed her husband, his daughters kissed him, the two young Cratchits kissed him and Peter hugged him.

"I'm very happy," said little Bob. "I'm very happy!"

"Ghost," said Scrooge, "I think our time together is almost over. Tell me, who was that man lying on the bed?"

The ghost took him, as before, into the areas of the city where businessmen worked, but at a different time, it seemed to Scrooge. In fact, there was no obvious order to these later scenes, except that they were all in the future. There was something the same about all of them, however: the ghost did not show Scrooge himself.

The ghost didn't stop for anything either. He just carried on, until Scrooge asked him to stop for a moment.

"This street that we're hurrying along," said Scrooge, "is

where my office is. I see the building. Let me see what I will be like in the future."

The ghost stopped but his hand pointed somewhere else.

"Why do you point over there?" asked Scrooge. "My office is this way."

Still, the hand pointed somewhere else.

Scrooge hurried to the window of his office and looked in. It was an office still but not his. The furniture was not the same, and the person in the chair was not him.

The ghost pointed as before. Scrooge joined him and they floated along the ground to an iron gate, surrounded by mist.

A churchyard. So the poor dead man lay under the ground and Scrooge would find out his name now. It was a gloomy, frightening place.

The ghost stood among the **graves** and pointed down to one. Scrooge approached it, trembling. He dreaded looking down.

"Before I look at the grave you're pointing at," said Scrooge, "answer me one question. Are these the shadows of the things that *will* be, or are they only shadows of things that *might* be?"

Still the ghost pointed down to the grave by his feet.

"Men can change the future if they change their behaviour," said Scrooge. "Tell me that's true!"

The ghost didn't move.

Scrooge moved towards the grave, trembling as he went. Following the ghost's finger, he read on the grave his own name, Ebenezer Scrooge.

The Last of the Spirits

"Am *I* that man on the bed?" he cried, on his knees.

The finger pointed from the grave to him, and back again.

"Oh no, no!"

The finger was still there.

"Ghost," he cried, holding its robe, "listen! I'm not the man I was. I will change, I promise. You wouldn't show me this if there was no hope for me, would you?"

For the first time, the ghost's kind hand trembled.

"I will celebrate Christmas properly and I will keep Christmas in my heart all year. I will live in the Past, the Present and the Future. The ghosts of all three will live inside me. I won't ever forget the lessons they taught me. Oh, tell me that the name on this grave can disappear!"

As he begged, he tried to take the ghost's hand in his, but it pushed him away.

Holding up his hands in a last prayer to save himself and alter his future, he saw the ghost, with its hood and robe, start to change. It got smaller and smaller, and finally it changed into a bed sheet.

Chapter 9
The end of it

Yes! The bed sheet was his. The bed was his. The room was his. And even better, he had time to make changes and improve himself.

"I will live in the Past, the Present and the Future!" Scrooge repeated, as he got out of bed. "The ghosts of all three will live inside me. Oh, Jacob Marley and Christmas time – thank you for this!"

Before, while was with the ghost, his face had been full of tears but now it was glowing with happiness.

Then he noticed the bed curtains. "They're still here!" he cried, holding them in his hands. "I can change the future. I know I can!"

He was so happy that he was laughing and crying at the same time. "I feel as light and happy as an angel," he said, in a carefree voice. "I feel as merry as a schoolboy!"

He ran into the sitting room. "There's the door where the ghost of Jacob Marley came in. There's the corner where the Ghost of Christmas Present sat! There's the window where I saw the ghosts floating in the air! It's all true. It all happened. Ha, ha, ha!"

For a man who hadn't practised for so many years, it was a brilliant laugh.

"I don't know what day of the month it is!" said Scrooge. "I don't know how long I've been with the ghosts. I don't know anything."

Suddenly, he heard the sound of church bells ringing, lots of them. Ding, dong. Ding, dong. Ding, dong.

He hurried to the window and opened it. He put his head out. There was no mist, no fog. It was a clear, bright, frosty day. The air was sweet and fresh and filled with the sound of merry bells.

"What day is it?" cried Scrooge, calling down to a boy who was in his best clothes.

"What?" answered the boy, looking up.

"What day is it, little boy?" said Scrooge.

"Today?" replied the boy, surprised that he was asking. "It's Christmas Day!"

"It's Christmas Day?" said Scrooge to himself. "I haven't missed it. The ghosts have done it all in one night. They can do anything they like. Of course they can. Of course they can." He looked out the window again. "Young boy!"

"Yes?" said the boy.

"Do you know the butcher's shop in the next street?" Scrooge asked.

"Of course I do," replied the boy.

"What an intelligent boy!" said Scrooge to himself. To the boy, he said, "Have they sold the huge turkey that was hanging up?"

"The one that is as big as me?" asked the boy.

"What a lovely boy!" said Scrooge. "It's a pleasure to talk to him. Yes, my dear."

"It's hanging there now," replied the boy.

"Is it?" said Scrooge. "Go and buy it."

"Are you joking?" said the boy.

"No, no," said Scrooge. "Go and buy it and tell them to take it to this address." He told the boy the address. "Go now and I'll give you a pound. If you come back within five minutes, I'll give you two pounds."

The boy ran off quickly. Scrooge had never seen a boy run so fast.

"I've given him Bob Cratchit's address," said Scrooge to himself. "The butcher's are going to send the turkey there." He rubbed his hands together and laughed merrily. "Bob won't know who sent it. It's twice the size of Tiny Tim."

Scrooge took out his best clothes and got dressed as quickly as he could. He found it very difficult to shave because his hands were shaking so much from excitement.

Finally, he went downstairs and to the front door. As he stepped out, he noticed the knocker. "I hardly ever looked at it before," cried Scrooge. "But I will love it forever! It's a wonderful knocker."

He started walking through the streets. They were full of people, as he had seen with the Ghost of Christmas Present. Scrooge gazed at everyone with a delighted smile. He looked so pleasant that three or four people said to him, "Good morning! Merry Christmas to you!"

He hadn't gone far when, coming towards him, he saw one of the charity men who had visited him in his office the day before. Looking at him, Scrooge felt a strong feeling of regret.

"Hello," Scrooge said as he approached the man. He took both his hands in his own. "Merry Christmas to you!"

"Mr Scrooge?"

"Yes," said Scrooge. "That's my name, and I suppose it's not a pleasant name to you. Please let me apologise for my behaviour yesterday. I'd like to give some money to your charity after all."

Scrooge told him the amount.

"Really?" cried the man, shocked. "That's a lot! Are you serious?"

"Of course I am," said Scrooge, smiling.

"Thank you!" said the man.

Scrooge carried on walking. He watched the people hurrying through the streets, wished children merry Christmas and gave money to people begging. Everything made him feel happy. He had never dreamt that any walk could give him so much pleasure.

In the afternoon, he walked towards his nephew's house.

He passed the door a dozen times before he felt brave enough to knock. But he did it at last.

"Is my nephew at home?" said Scrooge to the servant girl. A nice girl! Very.

"Yes, sir."

"Where is he, my love?" said Scrooge.

"He's in the dining room, sir, with his wife. I'll take you upstairs. Please follow me."

"Thank you," said Scrooge.

"Fred!" said Scrooge, as he entered the room.

"Who's that?" cried Scrooge's nephew.

"It's me, your uncle. I've come to have dinner with you, Fred."

Everyone was so surprised!

He was given a very warm welcome. In five minutes, he was sat in the most comfortable chair by the fire, a glass of mulled wine in his hand.

Everything looked the same as when he had seen it with the Ghost of Christmas Present. Fred's wife looked the same. And Topper, Fred's friend, looked the same. So did the wife's sister. It was a brilliant party, with brilliant games and lots of fun!

But Scrooge was early at the office the next morning. He needed to arrive first so that he could be there already when Bob Cratchit came in late! It was absolutely essential.

And he did it. Yes, he did! The clock struck nine. No Bob. A quarter past. No Bob. He was eighteen and a half minutes late. Scrooge sat waiting for him.

Bob took off his hat before he even opened the door. He took his scarf off too. He was in his little room in a few seconds and started writing straight away.

"Good morning!" complained Scrooge, in his usual angry voice. "Do you know what time it is?"

"I am very sorry," said Bob. "I'm late, I know."

"Yes, you are!" shouted Scrooge. "Come over here, please."

"I had a lie in. It's only once a year," said Bob, almost begging. He appeared from his room. "It won't happen again. I went to bed late last night because we were celebrating."

"Listen," said Scrooge, "I'm not going to accept this behaviour any longer. And so," he continued, jumping up from his chair, "and so ... I'm going to raise your salary!"

Bob felt very confused. He started trembling. He was sure that his boss had gone crazy and he was scared of him.

"Merry Christmas, Bob!" said Scrooge enthusiastically, as he put a hand on his clerk's shoulder. "I haven't given you a merry Christmas before, Bob, have I? I'll raise your

salary and try to help your family. We'll discuss it all this afternoon, with a big Christmas bowl of mulled wine!"

The clerk just looked at Scrooge, shocked.

"Make a bigger fire, Bob!" continued his boss. "That one is tiny! How can you keep warm with such a small fire?"

Scrooge **kept his promise**. He did it all ... and much more.

Tiny Tim did not die and Scrooge was a second father to him. He became a good friend to everyone, a good boss and a good man – in fact, the best in the city!

Some people laughed to see the change in him, but he let them laugh and didn't pay much attention. He was intelligent enough to know that people always find it strange when there is a big change like that. He laughed with them.

Yes, he kept his promise every day for the rest of his life. And he never saw the ghosts again.

People always said of him that he knew how to celebrate Christmas well, better than anyone else. Let's all try and do the same. And so, as Tiny Tim said, God bless us, every one!

THE END

VISIT MY WEBSITE

You will find:
- **information** about my **other books**
- **free stories**
- **free exercises** for this book
  (vocabulary exercises, comprehension exercises and notes about British culture)

ReadStories-LearnEnglish.com

MORE STORIES

A1+ Elementary

A2 Pre-intermediate

B1 Intermediate

B2 Upper intermediate

Words from the story

alter (v)
change

apprentice (n)
a person who is learning a job from someone skilled

bah humbug (exclamation)
a phrase used to show dislike or frustration, often about something happy or festive

bankrupt (adj)
unable to pay your debts; having no money

beg (v)
ask for something, especially for money or help

bell (n)
a hollow object that makes a ringing sound when you hit it

biting (adj)
very cold, causing pain

bless (v)
ask God to protect or help someone (**blessing**, n)

blindfold (n)
a piece of cloth used to cover someone's eyes so they cannot see

blind man's buff (n)
a children's game where a blindfolded person tries to catch others

carefree (adj)
without worries; relaxed and happy

carol (n)
a traditional song, sung at Christmas

cellar (n)
a room below ground level in a house, usually used for storage

charity (n)
giving help or money to people in need

clerk (n)
a person who works in an office doing simple tasks

crown (n)
a special hat usually worn by a king or queen, symbolising power

crutch (n)
a stick used to help someone walk, especially if they are injured

darkness (n)
when there is no light

day off (n)
a day when you do not have to work

dear (adj)
loved or important

debt (n)
money that you owe to someone

do somebody good (phr)
help someone feel better or improve their situation

drag (v)
pull something/someone along the ground with effort

dread (n)
a strong fear or worry about something in the future (**dread**, v)

emotion (n)
a strong feeling, such as happiness or sadness

enthusiastic (adj)
showing a lot of excitement or interest

festive (adj)
related to a celebration or festival, usually Christmas

frost (n)
thin ice that forms when it's very cold (**frosty**, adj)

funeral (n)
a ceremony for someone who has died

gaze at (phr v)
look at something for a long time

giant (n)
a very large person

goose (n)
a large bird that lives near water (**geese**, plural)

gloom (n)
darkness and sadness (**gloomy**, adj)

glow (v)
shine softly, often in the dark

grave (n)
a place where a dead body is buried

holly (n)
a plant with sharp, green leaves and red berries, often used as decoration at Christmas

hood (n)
a part of a coat or robe that covers the head

invisible (adj)
something that cannot be seen

keep your promise (phr)
do what you said you would do

knocker (n)
a metal object on a door used for knocking

lie in (phr)
stay in bed longer than usual in the morning

lit up (phr)
made bright with light

merry (adj)
happy, especially during a celebration like Christmas

mist (n)
a thin cloud close to the ground that makes it hard to see

mulled wine (n)
hot wine with spices, often drunk at Christmas

mutter (v)
speak quietly in a way that is hard to hear, often when you're annoyed

partner (n)
one of the people who owns a business and shares the profits

pudding (n)
a hot sweet British dish, often like a cake, made from flour, fat and eggs with fruit, jam etc in or on it

pyjamas (n)
clothes worn for sleeping

represent (v)
stand for or symbolise something

robe (n)
a long, loose piece of clothing

rub (v)
press and move your hand or an object over something

self (n)
used to refer to a person

servant (n)
a person who works for someone in their home, doing things like cleaning or cooking

shabby (adj)
in bad condition

slippers (n)
soft shoes worn indoors

snuffer (n)
a device used to put out (= stop) candles

sprinkle (v)
scatter small amounts of something, like water or powder

stare (v)
look at something or someone for a long time without moving your eyes

stingy (adj)
not wanting to spend or give money

strike (v)
show the time by making a ringing noise etc

terror (n)
extreme fear

toast (n)
a drink in someone's honour (**toast**, v)

torch (n)
a portable light that you can carry

torture (v)
cause great pain to someone, sometimes emotional pain, usually on purpose

tremble (v)
shake slightly because of cold, fear or excitement

unsettled (adj)
not calm; worried

vanish (v)
disappear suddenly

workhouse (n)
a place where poor people worked in exchange for food and shelter in the past

www.ingramcontent.com/pod-product-compliance
Lightning Source LLC
Chambersburg PA
CBHW011958090526
44590CB00023B/3777